T0104437

TATTOOED
—— WITH ——
TABOOS

An Anthology of Poetry by
Three Women from Northeast India

TATTOOED
— WITH —
TABOOS

An Anthology of Poetry by
Three Women from Northeast India

Chaoba Phuritshabam
Shreema Ningombam
Soibam Haripriya

PARTRIDGE
A Penguin Random House Company

TATTOOED WITH TABOOS

An Anthology of Poetry by Three Women from Northeast India

Copyright © 2015 by Chaoba Phuritshabam;
Shreema Ningombam; Soibam Haripriya

Cover Design: Kapil Arambam

First Edition: 2011

ISBN: Softcover   978-1-4828-4852-6
        eBook   978-1-4828-4851-9

Print information available on the last page.

To order additional copies of this book, contact
Partridge India
000 800 10062 62
orders.india@partridgepublishing.com

www.partridgepublishing.com/india

CONTENTS

ANGST FOR HOMELAND

LOVE AND LONGINGNESS

Shreema Ningombam

Chaoba Phuritshabam

Soibam Haripriya

For women on thresholds and beyond;
across space, time and borders

Preface

Manipur, a princely state before its merger with India on October 15, 1949 was a backdrop of the Second World War which was at that time locally known as Japan lan (war). In another obscure event in the history of India's freedom struggle Indian National Army ventured till Moirang, the very place where Khamba and Thoibi legend is rooted.

The rise of secessionist movement in various parts of the region has provoked one of the harshest militarisation from the Indian state. People have been bearing the effects of these tussles between the state and the non-state armed groups. The nude protest by twelve women on July 15, 2004 in front of Kangla fort against the rape and murder of Thangjam Manorama had left an ineffaceable picture on the minds of the outsiders within India and beyond. Ironically amidst all these turmoil the Northeast India is now harked on as an important "gateway" to Southeast Asia in the wake of India's Look East Policy.

But there is much more to the imagination and construction of the Northeast region. The case of Manipur is marked by continuity in a painful juncture. Irom Sharmila has been fasting for more than a decade in her struggle to repeal Armed Forces Special Powers Act (AFSPA). This peculiar circumstance has produced multifarious forms and themes of expressions. While its people have been trampled upon by socio-political turmoil; there is a multitude of dissenting voices both fearful and redeeming at the same time. The turmoil, ironically, has been churning out literature and various forms of art.

For many reasons not difficult to fathom, women have been made to surrender their individualities at the altars of socio-political violence and overarching patriarchal structure. There are many writing by women and on women but there is a dearth of avowed feminist literature in English coming from Manipur. This anthology would be an endeavour to fill this vacuum.

Introduction

This anthology records an angst of the times, developed within the consciousness of the poets. Circumscribed by the construct of womanhood, enveloped within the halo of love, betrayal and breathing, these poems are located in the setting of a conflict torn society. The poets use the personal as a tool to document the changing frames of society and its practices, which seem to be 'set in stone', through the metamorphosis of their moods, anxiety, hysteria and melancholy.

Certain sections of this anthology reflect the desire to trespass spaces denied to women in the personal as well as the public sphere. Womanhood is at all times projected as an image of the eternal mother whereby the poems try to resurrect the other women, the fallen. The poetry questions the accepted symbols of power while seeking within the body and without the inner core contained in being a woman, by virtue of which certain thoughts and feelings are deemed blasphemous if revealed. It is the exploration of a woman's self and her intimate feelings and emotions.

The anthology is thematically divided into three sections: 'Tattooed with Taboos', 'Angst for Homeland' and 'Love and Longingness'.

The section 'Tattooed with Taboos' rejoices in sexuality, desire and waywardness in an unbound way. It explores the pangs, sorrows and joys of being a woman who is made profane and sacred at the same time. Womanhood is usually portrayed through taboos and deification. The collection is written in celebration of the long overdue call for the detachment of morality from sexuality. Through words, the nuances of her thoughts and feelings are revealed and a demystification of the forbidden, the secret and sacred nature of the sexuality of women in our society, is attempted. Desire must be emancipated, washed and liberated from behind the veil, from mere whispers. Women's sexual desire must be recognized and conceived as natural act of fulfillment, not condemned through taboos placed on their clothing or in her wombs. There is no atonement for those who reject boundaries and ties. But then is it really necessary to seek redemption?

The section 'Angst for Homeland' looks at the dying landscape of a land of belongingness and seeks truth that seems like a mirage of an oasis in the wilderness. The wilderness that lures us and calls us when we are exiled still gives hope of gathering fragments for a new beginning. It depicts the irony of the homeland, being housed within an insatiable empire. The predicament here is of an emotional flux of our inability to love or hate, embrace or reject this land that we call our home. Somehow the trauma of our homeland seeps into our veins. The malady of this land is ours.

The section 'Love and Longingness' tries to grasp love which is akin to clasping sand on a shore. Love as love in itself is absolute, standing alone in its solitude neither connected to a person or an object, or to the memory of anything tangible. The pang that runs through these poems seeks this exhilarating emotion in its entirety. Love here is removed from hope and manifested as renunciation from birth and death.

The anthology captures the moods emerging like a wave from within – feelings of anguish, torment, exhilaration or a desire for certain uncanny elements which confirm our existence. The poems may stir a rebellious anxiety in each reader. One's thoughts can connect with the writings or go beyond its bounds. The moment poems are read, they sprout wings.

One Year of *Tattooed with Taboos*

A friend in a conversation narrated an anecdote where the members of his family in his son's *chaumba* (the ritual for the baby's first feeding of rice) objected to placing *Tattooed with Taboos* as the book, which symbolises knowledge, along with an assortment of elements placed in front of the child to choose from. These elements (earth, gold, silver, paddy, a tool, a book – *Tattooed with Taboos* which was eventually banished) signal the path the child would take in the future. In disbelief I asked him again if it was really so. He replied 'Yes I had to eventually evacuate Tattooed with Taboos'.

The cover of the first edition of *Tattooed with Taboos* has a piece of the hem of *phanek*, the traditional sarong like dress worn by the women in Manipur. The social matrix creates a norm which makes phanek 'untouchable' to the menfolk. The phanek of mothers, sisters and specifically of wives are not to be touched if the man wishes to retain his manhood and social dignity. Phanek is considered an inauspicious sign as it has the possibility of containing in it the residue of women's discharges. This was the precise reason why *Tattooed with Taboos* was evacuated from being a part of the ritual. A book with the cover of phanek cannot be tolerated, more so in the aforementioned ritual setting, it would be thought of as an affront. The book seems irredeemable. Yet it does not call for redemption. The cover of the book does not mean to emphasise the design and the fabric but the moral archaeology and anatomy of phanek in our society.

The anthology is in three sections: 'Tattooed with Taboos', 'Angst for Homeland' and 'Love and Longingness'.

The first section 'Tattooed with Taboos' deals with bodies and desire, the phrase seemed perfect to capture what we wanted to speak through the medium of poetry. Meitei society akin to other societies smothers in whispers issues of sexuality. Consequently vocabularies connoting acts of bodily pleasure are relegated to the category of dark things. Desire of the bodies remains condemned as: *amotpa* (dirt), *amangba* (impure), *choukhattaba* (uncivilized) etc. Though there is a convention of forbidden-ness, the valley of Manipur is rampant with dark corners of restaurants. People of this land have followed this dictum literally, thus sex and its paraphernalia- 'dark things' are done in dark corners of windowless cottages known in common parlance as restaurants. Such places dots the Tiddim Road, a perfunctory count in a distance of less than three kilometres reveal an approximate count of thirty such places vying for attention and alternately making futile attempts to be subtle.

Some newspapers carry picture of girls caught in compromising position in their semi-naked state and shirtless boys in such restaurants. But then the semi-naked women and shirtless boys do not carry the same disgrace. The moral weightage they carry is entirely different. The demystification of the secret as well as sacred nature of sexuality of women in our society remains the greatest predicament of our times. An irony is that men are proud to claim the renunciation of their celibacy yet women claim the strictly kept self-abnegation.

In many of the poems freedom of a different kind is imagined and sought for, freedom to kill oneself if one does not wish to live, freedom to disgrace oneself if dignity becomes too oppressive and freedom to fall into insanity if one no longer wants to rationalize the logic and norms and conventions.

We were asked time and again on our decision to publish the poem together and not alone. We met at a time of personal milestones. We knew of each other through articles and had a rough idea of our thinking. At one point of time we were all staying near University of Delhi campus. Eventually we ended up staying over at one place for days. Endless conversations led to many poems during this time but not with *Tattooed with Taboos* in mind. All of us used to write before but the coming together have been an important influence in our lives as well as our writings. It can be said that we shaped each other's thoughts through the sharing of erratic and painful changes in our lives. It was a year of many thoughts and intense writings. Some wounds festered into poems. This gave us a realisation of the importance of solidarity, a space to nestle together. Women's solidarity has been quashed time and again. It was essential for us to have solidarity to share common ideology and common concerns of our own body and choices we make over our body. The concern of society and politics of Manipur become fundamental as we have been a part of a society denied of basic human rights. We were confronted with the exigencies of our space and time where we thrive as female bodies. Then only we could get on with the acquisition that our bodies are in such a social and political matrix which marks our corporeal skins.

Oja Laishram Samarendra, a renowned poet of Manipur said on the World Poetry Day, March 21, 2013 in a function held in Jawaharlal Nehru Dance Academy, Imphal, 'Yumda leibiganuko, yumda leiba haibase mahapap ne. Yumda leidou saruk lamgi sha oina shikhibana henna phei' (Please do not stay in the house. To be confined in the house is the original sin. Rather than being in a house, it is better to die a beast of the wild). The city of Delhi is no less a wilderness. The city has mauled us, molested us, racialised us. The city hardened us like a calloused hand of a labourer; tenderness seems to have been lulled into sleep within us, making us women with sharp tongue, with bitter hearts. At the same time, we have rediscovered ourselves in the city, we saw from a distance an imagination of our home under the eastern sky, damned and loved at once. Almost the first two decades of our lives in Manipur could not make us understand our people, our land and our feud. It was only from a distance that we could see ourselves clear and sharp, our myopic eyes seems to have been cured. In a small godless corner of that city of wilderness we have talked, thought, cried, wailed, cursed, broke the spell and wrote many of the poems; wrote of a homeland we have not known completely which we still do not know. We have been told by one of the famous women writers of Manipur that we tried our best to know but we failed because we have not seen the land enough to own it even though it is now in an irresurrectible conditions, but she could see in us a desperation to know our own land vis-a-vis the constant alienation faced by us while grazing in that wilderness.

There are un-narratable tales of disappearance of many sons, husbands; violations of many women; mothers' nude protest in front of Kangla; conspiracies hatched to divide people; barbwire erected across the capital. So many tales – some grotesque, some fairytale, some real. However when we travel down the dusty road, the lanes of the villages through the bamboo groves life looks peaceful; where is the blood, the bullets or the Dark Law? One can't find violence in everyday banal hours, but we have at least once in a lifetime heard the bullets raining in the faraway hills, the pictures of mutilated bodies, stories of women violated, and of a single woman with medusaic hair fasting and being forced fed for more than a decade or so. In many of those smoky evenings, the hills swallowing the suns, the evening moon hung in the eastern sky of the past, we try to sniff the scent of that earth we have long forgotten, tried to dream in a desperate longingness for the cool breeze of Kwakta, the mythical residue of the folklore of Loktak. We tried to write of a land which we have forsaken for a decade.

Publication of the first edition of *Tattooed with Taboos* was during the economic blockade in Manipur for months in the latter half of 2011. Prices of all essential commodities rose phenomenally. LPG gas cylinder was sold in black market as high as Rs 1500 to Rs 2000; three to four times the normal price. The economic blockade is consistently used as a form of means of protest is what is called by many 'a weapon of choice' that is used to pressurise for multifarious demands. The longest in recent years would be the ninety two days of economic blockade in 2011 on the Sadar Hills issue. Protest against government in this multi-ethnic state often culminates into targeting the majority-community which is equated with the ruling government. On the other hand however working people of all ethnicities suffer and elites of all communities gain much from such mode of protests. It is not surprising considering the spoils that are to be shared. Neither the state nor the central government have made any real effort to deal with this crisis. In the 2011 economic blockade a litre of petrol was sold as high as Rs 200, three times as high as the normal price. The cost of the paper high even in normal circumstances (due to high transportation charges as Manipur is a landlocked state) rose phenomenally. Kangla Printers was kind enough to give us the paper in the normal price; they also provided the ISBN number. We had to publish it, the reasons for which are still incomprehensible to us. To many the choice of printing it in those politically charged circumstances was even more unfathomable. For us however there was a realisation that the anthology is not merely a book but a form of resistance to show to the entrenched systems of our world, an unconscious delusion that we wish to revolt even if it is through the means of some banal words, words are the only tools we were left with.

At times in a small corner of that wilderness we have shared meals from the same plate, drunk from the same glass, cursed from the same mouth, loved the land and man from our tiny heart, fissured and bleeding tears, we wrote the poems with all the vagaries of lives of three women growing into womanhood. Our poetry was written in at some times of our lives which we would not love to recall. We try to understand our homeland, express anguish in love and try to exorcise ourselves by scribbling poems. But our poetry will haunt us, we are doomed to read it again and again in various poetry meets which came and which are ought to come. It is a terrible task to revisit our shadows long abandoned. We cannot be exorcised from our poetry by any witchcraft when we ourselves practice heresy.

We cannot be more grateful to those who read our poems, who felt them and gave us feedback; we are more grateful to those friends who has criticised us, those few who took the anthology from us because they want to refer our book in their papers and research. We realise we have done something, a little thing.

Tattooed with Taboos

.

Soibam Haripriya

After the Wedding

The deed was done
Emptiness succeeded
After containing you in me
Void of withdrawal
Tired bedsheets soaked with violent sweat

At the break of dawn
I swept and swobbed
The strange courtyard of my eternal exile
Disguising bruises of yesterday's invasion
I knelt in front of the gray Tulsi
Desiccated by the merciful sun
Worshipping the dried remains
My forehead touched the earth
Lingering odour of cowdung –
Merged with the scent of mekruk

Containing the churning of my being
Thirsting to uproot and crumble
Those mute twigs of sacredness
My tears left five damp spots

♦♦♦

Tulsi: sacred basil
Mekruk: incense

Five Days' Untouchable

Is this blood of life
Merely to mark me impure
For Genesis says
I am not a creator, but created,
Created from a man?

For five days
Quarantined from the rest
By this unholy fluid
Wrapped with untouchable phanek
Phanek after Phanek
Carrying my untouchable-ness
Accursed piece of cloth
Contaminated for a lifetime

Neither nocturnal tryst nor daytime assault
Defiled the hands that tore it away
Yet lying apart from me
In the pale weather beaten bamboo polankhok
He watched the muga fabric
Soak up the rain
Droplet after droplet.

♦♦♦

Phanek: traditional clothing for women which covers the lower half of the body akin to a wrap-around. There is a taboo placed on seeing it hung on a clothesline before going out of home and the touching of the phanek by the husband is considered inauspicious in Meitei society.

Polankhok: a clothesline made of bamboo

Muga: silk

Are You Pleased

With your door
so low
I have to come
crawling on
my knees
I am walking
on all fours
Now,
are your pleased?
In chains
I am dragged
Free me
I cry
But
I am the one
With the jagged-teeth knife
in hand
I must kill
things
they taught
Unpeel
the layers
they painted
on me
I will melt
these windowless
icy walls
of love

Those
cauldrons
of lust
will
paint
your feverish
forehead
and you
will come
crawling
I will give in
no more
to promises
and sickly sweet
scented flowers
and glittering stones

♦♦♦

I Died a Little

I died a little
Killed by impure little droplets
Though there were celebrations
The stained cloth
Became my flag
I was congratulated
For reasons I knew not
My mother said
I was now a complete woman

I died a little
Killed by impure little droplets
Deflowered
He celebrated
Being the first
That became his flag
Worn proudly around his neck

I died a little
Killed by impure little droplets
That refused to trickle
On the wedding night
Condemned
His disappointment
Inscribed upon doors without eyes
The cold door knob
Refused to shake hands with me
Wooden, opaque, unseeing
And it slammed against the shivering frame.

◆◆◆

I, Icon

Droplets of carbonic acid
Clear the fume laden sky for awhile
Smog hangs in the air like a feeble verse
While they transgressed me in a diabolic rhythm
With a strange memory-less nostalgia
I wept at the putrid smell of flesh and fluid
Staring at the mouldy leaves
Amongst which I was cast away

I once had a name
Now I stand mutated by pride and pain
Amidst the acid rain
My tears became raging flames
The self, no more me
Yet my pain, they say, is my triumph
Now I am put up for display
Cemented on a pedestal
The icon of womanhood
Covered with pigeon's droppings in a park

◆◆◆

Green and Yellow Buses

With blood shot eyes
he rubbed wildly against
the shoulders of an old lady
with a hollow cough
bent with age
Oblivious of me and the crowd
collected together into a sweaty mass
in those green and yellow buses
with the uniform thought of reaching a warm home

I smirked, I stared
He went on his singular mission
suppressing his animal grunts.
The bus screeched to a stop
A bunch of fragrant white flowers
Undone from the lady's coiled grey bun
Lay trampled by innumerable feet
He broke into a lazy smile
Watching the world
Through a dirty panel of glass
Streaked with vomit
And ancient spats of betel nut juice
Extracted by tired mechanical jaws

I took home
A repulsive feeling of disgust
And bathed for an hour
Willing the crystal water
To cleanse those dirty window panes.

♦♦♦

His and Hers

A bigger face
a bigger strap
a smaller face
a smaller strap
For thick muscular hands
for thin slender arms
They said it is god-given
Big things for man
small things for woman
Titan had wrapped them up
With velvet cloth
perfect wedding gifts
His and hers

A bigger hand
Harder slap
leaving bluish purple marks
You get accustomed to.

Slender hands
To be wrung about helplessly
To welcome
a burn here, a cut there
As one her kind
Should get accustomed to.

And all these came
Packed in a golden box with velvet inside
The sturdiness of his, the softness of hers
God-given
Wrapped in skin and bones
Perfect gifts
for Hu-man- kind

♦♦♦

Green Kangkhand

I await
days to come
in vague chronology
of my own
For winter and autumn
to merge in hues of yellow and white
For summer to melt
black noons
of familial transgressions
With fear
rooted at the spot
his touch
my repulse
and the soft melancholic wail
from within
Ominous warning sign
that I lost a
self
under the cloud
of transparent green kangkhand
overlooking
the limp and lifeless stars
scorched from view
by the burning sun

Soibam Haripriya

The monotonous hum
of the off-white Orient fan
watching me
from the ceiling
Un-feeling my pain
He and the fan
continued in their motion

◆◆◆

Kangkhand: Mosquito net

Of Clothes and Robes

It hung from my waist
and caught the wind when I twirled
It was green
faded
handed down
from one cousin to another
Till it reached me
the youngest
Set off against the white of my shirt
I wore it everyday
They say it wasn't
Ours

Replaced by a green
without a waist strap
With no clear beginning
nor an end
The end was the beginning
and vice versa
I secured it on my waist
It did not catch the breeze
They did not ask me
Whether I wanted this 'freedom'
They did not ask me
Whether I wanted to uphold 'culture'
While my brother cycled to school
In his grey trousers
With leg space for his two limbs

It did not have a khamen chatpa border
It was not tailored
from a striped khudei
But yet 'his' it was
they were his trousers

♦♦♦

Khamen chatpa: a pattern imprinted on traditional dress
which is given as a reward by the kings to noblemen
Khudei: traditional daily wear for men

Apologies

I can no longer provide
the pleasure of plunging
into my soul
and twisting the emptiness within
like strands of solitary entrails

I can no longer
be vacuum
or palpable matter
of a strange kind
mutated to accommodate
all that you demand of me

I can no longer
be a sponge
and absorb
blue bruises
and discoloured sperm

The handle is in your grasp
You can still penetrate deeper inside
with your cold steel blades
But my being has overflowed
Oozing out a dark liquid
And I am
As cold as your steel blades

♦♦♦

Three Questions

Why did you give me
this irreparable world to inherit
Tainted with stains of history
the world is lost to my kind
Your gallant invoking of the mere two battles
fought by women
amuses me to no end
for you know not
I live and die fighting
innumerable ones everyday

Why did you give me
your cemented dogma
where subdued tender shoots of green
Struggle beneath
I am older than the seasons
I am the aged clump of grass
Taking root
Irreparably cracking the cemented courtyard
I die and sprout again

Why did you give me
This soft tissue
at my throbbing core
to break and bleed
at first contact
You judge me by this myth
I am younger than your myths
I will melt and mould
genesis and revelation
to a lump of nothingness
and mock the demise of creation

◆◆◆

Shreema Ningombam

Sublime

She filled her pockets
With pebbles of life
Just to go down into the waiting river
Like she was going back to a deep tranquil womb

She made breakfast for her daughters
Then came back to the kitchen
Just to put her head in the gas oven
Like the final retreat to maternal odour

She was the mistress of the world
One says 'they will eat her alive'
Yes, she was eaten and left
Naked and coiled like a foetus
Rebels without armour
Fermenting from wrenched guts
They are made sacred
Has the sacred ever been loved?
Rinsed with an unnamed anguish
Lathered with the purest betrayal
Washed with ethereal agony
Glowing with the dew of pangs
They became sublime
So sublime
They are
Forbidden to touch
Forbidden to love
Forbidden to rescue

They are goddesses
Destined to stand alone
In a temple filled with pungent prayers
With their crumbling stone limbs
Who knows a goddess' loneliness?
Who knows her hunger for earthy love?
Who knows her yearning to be mundane?
Who knows that goddesses too fear?
Who knows that stone also bleeds?
Who knows the mute does speak?
It is that you and I
Have no heart to feel
No ear to listen.

◆◆◆

One Last Time

One last time,
Let me be disgraced in front of those million eyes.
One last time,
Let me ruin myself from where there is no salvage.
One last time,
Let me be immoral that shames immorality itself.
One last time,
Let me go wild into the wilderness in search of an aphrodisiac.
One last time,
Let me taste the most hated of loves.
One last time,
Let me exile myself to a place of no return.
One last time,
Let my body be tattooed with all taboos.
One last time,
Let me enjoy the most wanton of all dreams.
One last time,
Let me show my nakedness to the tempting tempest.
One last time,
Let me be a mother without wedlock ever locking me up.
One last time,
Let me drink the poison of life and die just to live again.
One last time,
Let me be sinfully free …
One last time,
One last time…

♦♦♦

Seven Witches

Come let us gather
In the shadow of the sinister moonlight
Among the trembling noise of wolves
In the dense scent of Chini-Champra
In the sombre flared with will-o'-the-wisp
In the lustful croaking of frogs for mates
In the glow of fireflies
Stealthily…slowly…
Let no one know
Awake no one
For they will see
Our forbidden nocturnal processions
The un-seeable ritual,
The un-speakable words
The un-inhalable scent
In whisper …in smiles…
In our heaving breathe
We shall speak.
Once more let's conspire
Against them

In this full moon night the tide in my female being
Dashes against the shore of my womb
Now! Now! Who will hold this tide?
Who is that magnificent one?

Lo! That baby in the basket
Oh no! In which river is she letting it sail?

For it inherited only her name.
Now sisters! Let each of us turn into the father.
And give the baby seven fathers' name
Then would the world's greed be quenched?

Let's go and unfasten
The hinges of those locked doors
Behind which you will see them
In seething silence
Incubating warm ova of freedom

Secretly let's roam and see the vales
Where in the hearth of each home
They sing a lullaby to their children
A lore, a tale about us...
The seven witches are mistresses of this world'
We shall sing back
'Let's conspire against world's loyal wives'

Why worry?
For our lost inauguration
A dip in the lake above the Chingphu hill
All that is needed for
An ultimate restoration
The secret of all secrets
That wretched human females are deprived of
The trump that makes us win all battles
The mantra of our eternal victory
Shall be with us till another death
We follow the only law we know of
Mistresses never share secrets with wives

♦♦♦

Chini Champra: a kind of fragrant flowering tree traditionally the flower is used by women to decorate hair bun for aesthetic purpose.
Chingphu: a hill in Manipur

Unburdening the Dead Spirits

Oh! Kunti you are lucky
At least you know the father of your first born
Look at me
I do not know who he is
But I am sure of what he is not
He is not that magnificent sun
Nor is he wind
Nor the earth nor the fire
Nor the water nor the sky

He came and keeps coming
Yet each day I know him less
A formless
A scentless
A colourless being
Was he actually human?
That too I do not know

That night
The eternally locked doors of my maiden-room
Unlocked itself
That un-crossable line was crossed
That infinite interface
Between the earth and the ocean
That day they say
Some tiny spirits like 'prestige' deserted me
One after the other
I do not know

How many such dead spirits are needed to be freed
Before I free myself?

That night he embraced me
On the floor of that horizonless expanse
Darkness disrobed my clothes one after the other
With each piece of cloth rustled away,
Tiny spirits flew out from the branches of my body
Like eternally caged birds
Whose sky flew open with their wings.

Breeze grazed my lips
And they say my grace was gone
A hand of storm burnt on my bosom
And they say my shame was lost
The earth merged within me
They say I lost everything…
Then…
The smudged darkness of my eyes stained his shoulder
My dishevelled hair teased his cheeks
The rose of my lips
Shamelessly bloom on his fertile forehead
Our blood merged
I do not remember what covered our bareness,
That night
My phanek or his khudei!
I know not

Wicked womb forever loyal to its eternal betrayal
Yet for the first time I loved to be betrayed
I trump the eternal swindler of this world

For the first time this betrayal freed me
From those dead spirits
Named ...
Izzat
Leirangi-leinam
Chastity...
This ultimate union
Made me lose everything
I did not know it is so easy to lose my essence
My maiden body has to just swallow a luminous globe
I did not know it is so easy to lose everything
My maiden mind had to just spill a droplet of secret.

◆◆◆

Izzat: a Hindustani word which means 'dignity'
Kunti: In the epic Mahabharat, Kunti is the mother of the
Pandavas or the five sons. They are born of different father.
Leirangi-leinam: Manipuri phrase meaning the scent of flower.

Bronze Pillar and the Crystal Fairy

She dashed against the bronze pillar,
Just to be shattered as ever.
Just to be gathered as ever.
The lustre, the glow, the strength,
All that it is to her,
She is happy to dash against it,
As long as the fairy flies
The broken wings, the untold tales,
The perfect pillar, the imperfect beings
So this is your story.
So as I heard; so I am told.
This is not your world dear!
Come I shall drop you to your ethereal home,
Gather up your pieces, your wings
Make haste, before the storm comes.

♦♦♦

In Red

I shall recall once before the everlasting sunset
How beautiful it was to be red
Myself red
And the red sky of dusk
And I recall what I whispered
That evening in red
In the ears of the hill-echoes
'Where shall you take me tomorrow?'
Far away from that furry thing
I touched beside my bed in my nightmare
Far away from the unknown who stalked me
When sleep bound my limbs

I recall what I whispered
That evening in red
In the ears of the ripe sun
'Whom shall you take me to?'
The one who will answer all my queries
Like 'why have I come here?'
To tell me what I do not know
When I say 'I don't know'
Like why some are forsaken
While others shake the bars of prison?

I shall recall what I whispered
That evening in red
To the smoke of fresh burnt hay
'Where shall I go back now?'

And how much I wanted to say
'I do not want to go back
Let me stay right here in the midst of this meadow
Forever and ever
As long as I am red'
Until the green grass turned red and said
'No, you must go before the night turns red.'

♦♦♦

Untamed

My wayward mind
Thought the unthinkable
My wilful heart
Sensed the un-senseable
My disobedient feet
Walked the un-walkable
My untamed lips
Spoke the un-speakable
My mischievous ears
Listened to the un-listenable
My feral eyes
Saw the un-seeable
Yes I am untamed
With my heart out
Waiting for none
Telling none
Asking none
Alone all alone…
Let me search for Thoibi's khwangchet
It must surely lie in that far fringe of Moirang
Let me search for the last adornment
Around Mainu Pemcha's neck
Let it be my last adornment this hour
Let me trace Panthoibi's footsteps
And be one of her last metamorphosis
Let me search for a grain of Phouoibi
Just to drop it stealthily in the chengphu of my love

The mermaid will not stop swimming, even when
Her fins are severed
The sun will not stop climbing the mountain,
Even when the height haunts it
Flowers will not stop blooming,
Even when it is long fallen
Birds will not stop flying,
Even when their wings are stolen
And I will not stop living,
Even when I am long dead.

◆◆◆

Thoibi's khwangchet: Khamba-Thoibi are legendary lovers of
yore in Manipur whose love story is still narrated. Thoibi was
the princess of Morang Kingdom and Khamba was an orphan.
Khwangchet is a kind of clothe used by women as a waistband.
Moirang: An ancient place in Manipur famous as the backdrop
of the KhambaThoibi legend
Mainu Pemcha: a legendary woman who committed suicide
by hanging herself
Panthoibi: a legendary woman who has many metamorphosis,
like Phouibi who is the goddess of grain
Chengphu: a large pot kept in the kitchen of every household
of Meitei community in which rice grain after husking is
stored ready to be cooked.

The Other Revolutionary

She took up Irabot's sickle
To chop off the overgrown beard
On her mother's chin
She too is a revolutionary

The wicked wind licks lecherously
Her thighs along which the phanek slithers
Yielding to the wanton wind
The phanek prostrate on the wayside cried
'Hey lady!You have dropped me'
She knowingly did not look back
She too is a revolutionary

The evening prayer to Sanamahi was offered
Forgetting her crimson lunar cycle
Only to remember when her man rush her phanek
From her waist that drunken night.
As the faint scent of haeme whiffs along
She too is a revolutionary

She rode away in the air
Screamed with muffled mouth
Forgot when she ought to remember
Swam in the clouds...
She thinks a thought
She too is a revolutionary

That night in that bloody war
A seed of revolution was sown
In her ravaged womb
Against law, against time
Against all dimensions of life
A revolution grows in her belly.
She is a revolutionary through the ages

♦♦♦

Irabot: a communist revolutionary of Manipur in the beginning
of the twentieth century
Sanamahi: the most important household deity of Meitei
society

The Eye

Behind the gaping door,
You stand silently and watch all
Thinking none watches you
And none knows you
You saw all
But you didn't see one thing
That your lover is in the fallen's arms
And she in his dream
You saw all
But you never saw how she wished to suck in her veins
All the poison of this world
And be silent
Forever silent on that lonely chair
You saw all
But you will never see
That there is a maibi in me
Who wishes to rebel every full frenzied moon
With her profane wizardry

You saw all
But you will never see
The one killed and buried in her backyard
When the whole world searches for him
Blaming those who roam in nights
But I see you…all through
There are eyes
In the breeze that rustles your locks
In the curtains through which you peep

In the hem of phanek
Eyes of the fallen
Of the irredeemable

◆◆◆

Maibi: a priestess in Meitei society who is also a fortune teller
and a healer

In Defiance

Let me cast aside these jewels
The adornments in my ears; the golden rope around my neck
Who am I waiting for to be watched with such longingness?
For whom am I waiting with such a burden?

Let me cast aside the inner layers beneath my phanek
Let my blood flow along the smoothness of my thighs
With a freedom that it has never known
Beyond all shame, let it be seen by all.

Why are my breasts being bound with such tightness
Is it the crime of shedding maternal milk?
They say it's a pair of divine beauty.
Divinity! Oh you always come with chains

Who has thrown me a piece of veil?
Veil be cast aside,
It is your gaze, it's your sense
What have my veil and I got to do with it.

I touched your feet that day in public
Now in this silent night you kiss my feet
Tell me whose feet are pure and who's impure,
Tell me, what is this purity?

Shreema Ningombam

A dip in the Ganges of sin
A silent confession in front of a sinner
A marriage solemnised by an illiterate priest
A purity made of all impurities

◆◆◆

To the Ema Lairembi

Mother, in this courtyard of yours
I am not allowed to offer floral tribute
It is my third day
And your carnival will be over today
Mother, answer me once!
Have you never felt that blood in your palm?
That warmth; that scent
You are a deity so are you free from this flow?
They say we are your daughters
They say we are your sons
How can we celebrate your flourishing procreation?
Without your bountiful blood
I, a maiden mother
An unsolemnised wife
Yet my mapannaiba phanek will not be waist up tonight.
Mother, would you begrudge my presence in your courtyard?
When you do not why would they?
Mother, tell them
We are your children
Neither pure nor impure
Neither full nor empty
Neither true nor false
Just beings

◆◆◆

EmaLairembi: Mother Goddess.
Mapannaiba phanek: a phanek with stripped lines of black
and another colour. The phanek is tucked around the bosom
by married women in rituals.

One Thousand and One Nights

I do not wish to tell you stories
To deter my death
One thousand and one nights no! No!
Save me from that
I just want one night
You writing stories on my body
With the pen of your fingertips
With the ink of your passion
Just one night
One night of our story
Not told by lips not written in letters
Just the scent of our skin
The mingling moisture of our breath
Just one night
Let's stain the white sheet of morality
With our common fluid
Although there is no going back
Let me try going back ....gathering
The remnants of our ultimate celebration
Of making a life
A life within another life

Remnants,
The stained phanek
The mark of your teeth on my bosom
Yet peace on my face
A strange scent on my body
The day after

I set forth to give up
Not only my life but,
All those illusions
Betrothed to me
At the moment of my birth
The birth of a woman

♦♦♦

Chaoba Phuritshabam

The Maiden Mother

Are you the hidden vines
Among the bamboo grooves?
Lost in the world with none to cherish
Are you the flower in the hills?
Fallen and unseen
Are you the enduring leibaklei?
Unafraid of being trampled and disgraced?
Or the 'ownerless mallika'?
The fallen one with none to gather the petals
When strewn astray?
Is she the kundorei?
Whose gaze ebbs away from her home?
Is she the singarei
Thrown midway before her bloom
Is she the thaballei that unwraps in the midnight?
In fear of the world's disdain.

◆◆◆

Mallika, kundorei, singarei thaballei are all names of flowers

Sati

Why wail?
Listening to the praise of the populace
It is said you are the daughter of Devi
The incarnation of goddess
In the lineages to come
Your fame shall remain
You are after all Sati
In the scorching separation
The wrath of fire was put to trial
Why lament?
Why do you not pride in yourself?
In the lineages to come
Your fame shall remain
You are after all a Sati

Following your footsteps
Putting up with judgmental eyes
Many a woman endured the rage
Of her husband's funeral pyre
In the lineages to come
Your fame shall remain
You are after all a Sati

Your sister Meikibi trailed your path
Defeated in the test of flames
Neither able to die
Nor able to live
Defamed and disgraced

From the unfathomable depths of her heart
Sati wails

She heard my metaphor
She knew my whining at last
She began narrating her heart's tales slowly
"I followed my slain husband
I thought of leaving the world
Overwhelmed by its oppression
Why defame me?
Why call me a Sati?
I am not a Sati
Who desires to be a murderer?
Am I glorified to make martyrs of more women?"
Thus wails the lady
With dishevelled hair
In rags;
She screams
"I am no longer Sati; I am not a Sati.
You traded my corpse with tradition?
Why call me a Sati?
In the altar of my last rite you want to sacrifice more women
I left this world; I could not bear the oppression
Why kill others in my name, no more! No more!
I am no longer that Sati
I am not a Sati
I don't know its meaning
I am not a murderer!"

◆◆◆

In Manipur there is a legend of Sati Khongnang and Meikibi Khongnang. Meikibi wanted to be a Sati but she could not bear the flames so she tried to run away but she was eventually forced into the funeral pyre of her husband. She was ridiculed and defamed for her cowardice. It is believed that the khongnang (banyan tree) still bears the mark of half burnt state

Midnight Monsoon

Like those millions in solitude
Peeping through leaves of memory
Buried inside my earthen heart
I lay myself in trusted arms
When the night falls asleep

Like those millions in silence
I left living
Beneath the paternal sun who veils your view
No one took a note on my departure
When the moon swallowed me in her seas

Like those millions in melancholy
I would sing love songs every midnight
As those disgraced reapers
Calling lost loves
Far in the hamlet

Like those millions in heaven
I bathed with sweet petals
With a thoughtless smile
I was led
To the forest of aphrodisiacs
While the hands of spring
Made the woods of April bright

Like those million tribes
Celebrating the agony of love
Wither midst the falling dew of shame
I am now in my crowning hour
No more I am
Those modest flowers

Like those million lofty blooms
Flaunting high in the virgin air
I'm back to those pathless forests
Searching for him again
Through the moonlit plain
When the midnight monsoon washes all my sins

◆◆◆

Fruits of Your Taste

Some have more curves
Some look fair and attractive
Yeah welcome to the market of fruits
You have the choice to hold and weigh
You can just lift and taste their juices
How far can fruits cry of your misdeeds?

Welcome to the market of fruits
Some are like your favourite apple
Some look like your juicy orange
You have choices in front of you
Apples, oranges, grapes,
Choose one of your own
Till the time market is open for you
You have the choice to hold and weigh
You can just lift and taste their juices
How far can fruits cry of your misdeeds?

♦♦♦

When Moirang Khamba
Met Krishna

He must be shouting for his roots,
He must be craving for his tribe,
He must be asking *machem Khamnu*,
Where he was born
Where he belonged
Mathura or Moirang?

I dreamt of pure love
Like that of Khamba-Thoibi
The eternal sacrifice of two lovers
I listen to the *Moirang-Parva*
To get a glimpse of their love story

I weep for *Khamnu*

Oh! how she suffered
Oh! how she nurtured *Khamba*

I crave for the courage of *Thoibi*
Who defied decrees for Khamba
Outwitting Nongban

But it was a famous poet
Who bewildered me
In another myth
Quite afar from what I heard
I remember my grandma telling me

The story of *Khamba-Thoibi*
I still am mesmerised
With the beauty of *Thoibi*

The epic poet
Retold the tale
How *Khamba* met *Krishna*
How they played the *Ras Lila*

Krishna reincarnated as *Khamba*
Ventured to Moirang
Then when I lost my way
I saw *Radha*
Playing Holi with *Khamba*
Khamba courting the Gopis

I pursue that myth
To my root
I question that history
Still it cannot answer
Where Khamba belonged?
Where he meet Krishna?
How he played the Ras Lila
In front of Thanjing Mandap!

Oh! Poet come back
And answer me
You have to re-write your epic
You have to re-sing the *Moirang-Parva*
I'm still waiting
How would you explain

Khamba playing holi with Radha
And flirting with Gopis

Oh! Poet come back
Console *Khamba's* lament
For the made-to-believe myth.

♦♦♦

Machem: sister
Mathura: birthplace of Krishna
Moirang: birthplace of Khamba
Khamba - Thoibi: legendary lovers in Manipur folklore.
Khamnu: Khamba's elder sister who raised him up as both were
orphans. Nongban pursued Thoibi. The folklore is recollected
in narration of Moirang Parva
Holi: the festival of colors in Hindu tradition
Gopis: lovers of Krishna
Radha and Krishna: Krishna is a Hindu god and Radha is
his consort
Ras lila: a dance played by Krishna and his Gopis
Thangjing Mandap: the courtyard of the diety Thangjing

Questions on Her

Fish evacuated Loktak
Smoked bullets fill her empty lubak
She recalls the face of her crying child
Waiting for her to come home
With handful of rice and hope...

The day falls mercilessly
Leaving her alone amidst the darkness
She couldn't get even a morsel to feed
Those hungry stomachs

In the middle of the Loktak
Who cheats her for so long
Embracing her only namesake pride
Lost and left
Only with her flesh
To be bidden and sold

Finally she closed her eyes
Murmuring and moaning in silence
'Is it me or the Loktak?
Tell me
Who is the real prostitute to you?'

◆◆◆

Lubak: it's a basket made of bamboo splits
Loktak: a large freshwater lake in Manipur

Angst for Homeland

Chaoba Phuritshabam

Between Two Flags

One, three headed
One, a charming chakra.
Scramble for me
I, bewildered
I, baffled
Beloved, both
Belonged to both
One, borne
One, nurtured

Frequent, my mind's eye
The flag embellished
With sakok
My thought feebled
At the flags' awaiting

Frequent in my thoughts
The flag embellished
With chakra
My thought feebled
At the flag
I didn't belong to

Mislaid at the warfield
Between two flags
I asked all
Who do I belong to?
Frequent in my thought
Can I belong to both?

One, borne
One, nurtured
I feared
Life's lofty forts
I feared
I couldn't traverse
These chained heights
I feared
The sakok embellished flag
Chasing me
With a sword
Stating a stranger, I am
Between two flags
Scrambling for me
She is mine
She is mine
They said
Sliced me
Some pieces for one
Some pieces for another
Why the scramble?
Who do I belong to?
Pacified myself
I, adrift
Between two flags
Between these two flags

◆◆◆

Chakra: the wheel in Indian National flag
Shakok: the head of animal, used in flags to symbolise ferocity
and valour of the various clan amongst the Meiteis of Manipur.

Freedom

In an empty room
In the midst of darkness
I seek the meaning of freedom
I cannot rule with guns in my hands
Nor can I defend with an army
Nor did I learn
The way Thangal General diffused the bomb
With a sway of his sword

In the midst of darkness
I seek the meaning of freedom
I wish like the brave Tikendrajit
At times I worry for this tiny soul of mine
This life envied even by Brahma
How can I lose it so easily?

If grand Paona was alive
Would I have been brave?
I ponder in the midst of darkness
Ceaselessly seek the meaning of freedom

In the distant hills and vales
The sounds of guns
Falls ceaselessly like July rains
Intruding my thoughts
Whose freedom are we seeking?
Is it for the Shiroy lilies in the hills?
Or for the Nong-een that waits for the moon?

Taamna that sings in the hills
Left the nest in fear of invasion
Tracing its path with its gentle voice
Shiroy in the hills no longer blooms
In fear of being plucked before time
Indeed it must have asked in spite of being mute
"Where is our freedom?"
I sit alone in the midst of darkness
Seeking the meaning of freedom
None comes to ask; none comes to tell
The meaning of my freedom

In the wake of revolution
The clear water of Loktak in shame
Veils itself with Phumdis
In the rhythm of ripples above Loktak
Flock of swans no longer sways in dance
Exiled from this Meitrabak of Porei
Beyond the fathom of vision
The sun sulks and no longer play

In the depth of Loktak
Thoughts somersault
Whose freedom is being sought?
Is it for the Siroy lilies in the hills
Is it for the Taamna of the hillside?
Is it for the veiled face of Loktak as well?
Whose freedom is being sought?
Once more the thought comes
This life that we get only once
This life that is envied by Brahma himself

Like Nong- een gazing at the trail of moon
Shall I waste away seeking the meaning of freedom?

◆◆◆

Bir Tikendrajit: a Manipuri Prince and Thangal general was the general of his time.
Paona Brajabasi: a martyr in the Anglo-Manipuri war at Khongjom in 1891
Shiroy: state flower in Manipur.
Taamna, Nongeen: kinds of birds.
Brahma: the Hindu god of creation
Porei: a king in ancient Manipur

Patriot of my Land

His head jammed with the smoke of cigars
His mouth foul
With expensive English wine
Once I encountered
The patriot of my land
Walking upon the muddy and bloody road
The day was dim and foggy
I couldn't see clearly
It looked like a dream
Though it was real
I regretted meeting him
The patriot of my land
Shouting on the road
Protesting with naked slogans
Written in RED BOLD letters
Copied from '60s western philosopher's book
'I'm breaking the law of dictators'
He sought poor people
We believed and followed
Another victorious day
He becomes another dictator
For the same poor people

◆◆◆

Operation Summer Storm

On the day of Cheiraoba,
My eyes were stirring
The empty vessel in my kitchen
Hurling at them many questions

Illusions of a yet to be miracle
Ruptured with my son's hunger
Seeking my gaze
I was looking at the dark empty road,
A miracle would come my way.
Why I'm living on this earth?
Lost in my own thought
The cry of my child woke me up again,
The tired corpse of my husband
Lay on the cold muddy floor.
He hides his pain and anguish
Over nothingness,
Over his own faith,
His eyes were red and wild,
Stare at me and laugh at me
Mocking my illusions of a yet to be miracle
He was laughing at me for the reason I was looking for,
Why am I still living on this earth?
Silence was broken again with the cry of my child

♦♦♦

Operation Summer Storm: A combing operation conducted in
Loktak Lake to flush out "insurgents".
Cheiraoba: New Year of Meitei community in Manipur

Shreema Ningombam

Mother

You were everywhere,
Yet I searched for you.
In the places of carnivals,
In the deepest of woods,
In between the locked horns of the wilds,
Among the cries of the flags,
Among the phantoms of the nights

I came home.
I found you.
In the nearest corner of my heart,
Peeping behind the curtain of my mind,
Playing with the music of my soul,
Beating the drum of my pulse,
Dyeing the crimson of my blood,
Swimming in the breath of my life

Some say you are a witch.
Some say you are an angel.
They say you are damned.
They say you are divine.

I came home,
To salvage your grave,
Where I found
The skull of my ancestor,
The naophum of my ancestral kin,
A torn phanek stained with her primeval blood,

An old chest that opens
With the faint smell of ancient breath
Tonight I light the light of my heart.
Prostrate in this vast graveyard,
With pride or with guilt I do not know,
Should I carry another mortal being in my womb?
I, a nameless mother wait and wait,
To mourn the death of my yet unborn.

◆◆◆

Naophum: a pot in which placenta is stored and buried in the backyard of a house. This is a custom in Meitei (Manipur) society but with the advent of urbanization this practice has dwindled.

Blooming

Peach blooms
It is the age of doom
Gone is the elephant's tail
It is time for disdain
Shangbrei blooms
It is time for carnival
Bunch in the bun blooms
It is time for the fallen flowers
Wildfire blooms in the slopes of hearts
It is time to wait
For the one who will never come

◆◆◆

Shangbrei: a kind of flowering tree

Fading Landscape

Something fades on this dying landscape
Is it a bonfire or a glow worm?
Perhaps a soul or just the tip of a cigar
Each night something burns to live
Each day someone always departs
Launching soul to starry sky
From peculiar places
Not aero, not terra or aqua
From something like blooming bosom
Sultry tresses...
Maternal sacs...

Once more a day has come
But not Monday or Tuesday
Just a day;
Unqualified; undefined
Neither dark nor bright but grey,
Like the trailing hair of an old witch
Not a song or a shrill just a droning hum
Like a swarm of bees from the hive of a heart
Ready to sting to death the gods among us
Oh! Poor bee-stung swollen god

Leaving queries unanswered
Once again the day has left like any other day
Like a half un-drunk glass of red tea on a tray
Like swallowing shadows
Erecting more monstrous ones

Just to write with a bolder ink
Again and all over again
Yet the image of old letters rises
Like a mirage in wilderness
Tempting, teasing, loving
My soul was the sole witness
Of my defeat in the hands of the wild
I yielded so that I do not regret
What I did; what I do or what I will ever do

No canon, no norm just the swaying leonine mane
No paradigms; no parameters
Only the measureless chase of prey
No fence; no borders just a grand gate
No judgment; no redemption
Just the lick of wild tongue on my face
And we are the worms from eagle's beak to chick's mouth
The owl of Minerva no longer flies over this land
White dove turns red
Yet this land harbours no regret
Wildly fresh as ever I chose to be here forever

♦♦♦

Rainbow

Violet leibaklei pierces the earth
Many a summer ago when she once walked this vale
Its faint scent opens its eyes whenever I close mine
Her dim soul glows whenever I look at a lazy distance
On the way back I saw her soul slowly descending and rising
With the waves of the archaic wind
In the autumn air
I saw it nestled in the cradle of a weightless leaf

Indigo sky mocked at me
As I once tried to play with the clouds
At last I played with pebbles and marbles
As if there would never be a game after
It was the morning that went and never came
Although I waited for the final game
On the way back I saw it between the human bulls
In the muddy battlefield
I saw them rolling in the mud

The flower from my hair
Fell and trampled in dust and foot
That day when I first came out of my home
Seeking a strange freedom in that seized street
On the way back I saw freedom curled asleep like a street dog
In the garden
I saw it playing hide and seek between the folds of the foliage

Green moors of this valley beckon me
Whenever I am exiled from this land

Calling me for the last truce
'As you killed my son give me your daughter'
And I shrugged and said so as you say
On the way back I saw her son playing with my daughter
From dreamy mountain
I saw their love melting down in ravines.

Yellow November fields opened themselves for visitors
Who were never ever inheritors.
Wild herbs; shrubs; half sun baked cow-dung and snails
Their sole heritage from this soil red with their kin's blood
On the way back I saw the visitors performing their daily rites
In the field I saw their dreams opening pearl-less oysters

Orange suns deliciously drooped on my courtyard
I plucked them one by one
One for me; one for the unknown; and one for the unnamed
I put them in the jar of my anguish
On the way back I saw suns getting burnt
In the jar I saw them melting into warm rays

Red cheeks of that summer beauty
Blushed by the unruly highland wind and Orion's luring gaze
At last they fled with her beauty
And the lovelorn searched for the stolen
On the way back
I saw her beauty kneeling at the tomb of the slain
In the grave I saw it walking every evening like a lost ghost

◆◆◆

Leibaklei: a flower that burst forth from the earth

One Day, Ema

One day, Ema!
It will rain
And you will unbind hair and wash it
In the slow dripping from the thatch
One day
Flowers will bloom
In your dark mystic bun
As if they were never plucked
One day
Wind will carry
The scent of your fresh steamed rice
Through the corners of this ravaged street
One day
They will come
Whom you have waited for so long
In this life or in this death
One day
The rainbow will colour
The ashen shawl around your bosom
With your darling shades
One day
Your children will fling open
The eternally closed gates
With the calls Ema! Ema!
One day
Kites will fly
In your blue sky with tails of freedom
With no one to harness them with a string

One day
I will garland around your neck
The wreath so painstakingly woven
As you walk past the triumphant crowd
One day, Ema!
One day…

♦♦♦

Broken

I am home and they are still here
These streets still scarred
These hills still in reverie
Which one is more sore?
The broken strings of your guitar
Or the broken notes of their Pena

This is the hour for wounds and maiming
There will be a time for mending and healing
There will be hours for mantra and magic
I wait for the Maibi
Who feels the meagre pulse on my wrist
And tells the fortune of this land
She tells over my body
The fever of this land
My pulse, the broken throb of our antique drum
My bosom, the angst of a missed progeny
My forehead, the warmth of a fresh pyre

The malady of this land is mine

This home gave us everything
A corner to live and die
A corner to croon and sigh
Though it could never give a tiny corner
To rest at long last
Broken bones of our hearts

◆◆◆

Pena: an indigenous stringed musical instrument

A New House in a New Country

He said he will build a farm house
I said I will give him the land
He said it will be called 'liberation zone'
"Man, Come there is a dustbin you can put down the gun"
Come have a drink, there are bottles you can carry on"
I said man can lay down guns and liberate himself.
What shall a woman lay down to liberate herself?
Yes he remembers the story I read
A new house in a new country
A house of windows
Through which we watch together
Beyond the beyond,
Horizon after horizon, sunset after sunset
Tune after tune...after the return.
You and I shall walk again on the wet fields
With a grotesque aluminium bucket to pick snails
Mossy with years of hibernation
Like our seasoned revolutionaries
You and I shall walk again on the evening lanes
Across the drowsy villa
Your thumb paints the colour of nongjabi
On my lips
From the shades of western vista

Will there be words left?
Will there be time that betrays?
He will love my old smile
Like he loves the old wine
Brewed with Sekmai water

◆◆◆

Nongjabi: the colour of sunset in the evening clouds.
Sekmai: a village through which Sekmai Turel (river) runs

Soibam Haripriya

... and We Leave Patches

What do I tell you
how it is
when from a distance
I watch the evening
dark and deep
fall
into the arms of day
The sun recedes
in the deep embrace
of the brooding hills
Then you arrived
to divide up
our lot
Yours and mine
Divide up
embraces
How is it?
How do we
cut apart
this book
we wrote
with stars
and half a moon
How do we
divide
conversation
Was it yours or mine?
A question

to my answer
An answer
to my question
Would the sun
not wait for dawn
Would the hills
not wait for dusk
What do I tell you
how it is
How do we
divide
you in me
me in you
And we leave
patches
in
what we wove
each carrying
a tattered bit
What do I ask now?
Would we seek
another loom
another thread?
or take our tattered bits
towards where
the brooding hills
embrace the sun?

◆◆◆

The End

This is where
the road ends
tarmac
of India Shining
gives way
to gravel
and red dirt
of India whining
Red eyed lantern
with irregular wicks
cast their sorrowful gaze
on the cables
above the village
Traversed
without stopping by
It would shine
in other places
Those islands of hope
a granary
of surplus
doesn't sow
but reaps
Oh how
is it?

♦♦♦

Soibam Haripriya

Another Polish for My Nails

promises and promises
give it a miss
It's unsure
why
you promised me the moon
and doted on my nails
the black stain of your promises
I live with the regret
Yet another five years
Optimist that I am
you will find me yet again
lining up in the queue
amongst stones and dust
of the rumbling school
roofless from your promises
waiting for the stain
secretly folding your promises
sliding it down
the box of dreams of democracy
locked securely for another five years
is lies and lies and lies
Yet I believed
like a love struck luckless lover
I wish I had chosen
another polish for my nails

◆◆◆

September Still

August auburn leaves
still fresh in my memory
Yet time has swallowed everything
Debris between time and I
Dreams ended somewhere between a gnarled tree
bursting forth into blooms of frangipani
and a marshy algae pukhri
I looked for a reflection in the pukhri,
a green layer looked back

The month of Mera,
lanterns hanging atop a single stalk of bamboo in the
courtyard
Quiet sky and September is still
Dried crisp yellow strands of sharp bamboo leaves
Make a grazing sound against a rare flutter of breeze
which manages to break through the grove of concrete.

The lantern always looks so cold a few hours into the night
Oil-less and ashamed
Its brother- the langmei in the hills
Still bright and fiery
Till all dies down in cinders
against the break of dawn.

◆◆◆

Mera: This is the month of October in Meitei lunar calendar
Langmei: fire in the hills for clearing forest for Jhum cultivation
Pukhri: Pond

111

Fragments

In you I see fragments
To write and write again
Lines like the furrows
where farmers plough
To plant seeds of steel
Breaking open your bosom
With spades of iron
To bring forth rains of steel

In you I see fragments
To weep and weep again
To rejoin the weeping river
That resembles a drying drain
Carrying with you the stench of the city
by the grand Bazaar

In you I see fragments
Of hungry souls
Where fire died
from hearths
to kindle in hearts

In you I see
Fragments and only fragments
The whole departed
And so will the fragments

◆◆◆

Join Magazine Secy

In red
Deep left red
On the straw stuffed mud wall
He wrote:
Join RPF
Another
Crossed it out
and wrote KYKL
The last
A hasty scribble
A witty retort
when in
advertising thus
for Kangleipak
A patrolling van's headlights
Shone on the mud wall
And he perched
Uncomfortably
Nailed between
the black sorok nalla and the mud wall
Cornered thus
He wrote in red:
Join Magazine Secy

♦♦♦

RPF, KYKL: non-state armed groups in Manipur
Kangleipak : an archaic name for Manipur Valley
Sorok nalla: roadside drain

Beginning

I am beginning
to forget
the taste of your lips,
the salt of your skin,
your face of blissful anguish

I am beginning
to forget
the tarmac of your roads,
the nectar of your rains,
the moon of your clear skies

I am beginning
to run
from the grip of your embrace,
from your heady thunder,
from your patriots
and your numerous lovers

I am beginning
to chase you
from the altar I built,
from the idols I installed,
from the tulsi of my courtyard

I am beginning
to pray for another chain

♦♦♦

Nambul Turel

Noisily
It flowed
In darkness
Of deep nights

Descending into the deserted city
of porous amnesia
Raindrops slither unwilling
crystal droplets
merge with
the monochrome of dark liquid leftovers

We discarded the fluid waste
And threw away
the dried crumbling bunch of forgotten roses
whose stench had
no memory of the red fragrance of love

We washed away ages of delusion
and brought in a new river
of meandering sparkles
And it rained crystals that night

◆◆◆

Turel : River

Lets Play

Lets play
A game
Your state and my corporation
Weld them
To force minerals
Out of rivers
To force Bauxite
Out of hills
To force timbre
Out of forests

Lets play
A game
Your words and mine
To force people
Out of homes
To force farmers
Out of fields

Let's play
A game
On this checked chessboard
Let's stake the lands
and the tutelary deities
Let the river run dry
To quench our thirst

Let the mountains spew gold
To satiate our hunger
And when the earth is squeezed dry
Let us stake the universe
And the planets

♦♦♦

My Friend

We met and how
Amongst fallen Gods and men
Amongst yellowed autumn
Promises of spring did sprout
When we melted frost with tears

We met and how
Amongst fallen monuments
Amongst broken shrines
Promises of revolution did germinate
When we grew our seeds of madness

We met and how
Amongst concrete walls
Amongst green tulsi
Promises of mayhem did soar
When we refused to stoop

We met and how
Amongst womb-less ancestors
Amongst untouchable phanek
Promised that you and I
Will re-write creation again

Love and Longingness

Shreema Ningombam

The Last Exchange

Do not go away so soon
Share with me your last secret
Before the evening bell rings
In the temple of this hazy hamlet
Come let us have our last exchange

Do not go away so soon
Share with me this last slice of green mango
Let me feel the shiver of sourness in your chin
In the orchard of this forbidden flora
Come let us have our last exchange

Do not go away so soon
Share with me this hay-fire
Before the last winter ends
Let us talk of you and me
Come let us have our last exchange

♦♦♦

Your Coming

Every ladder I climbed so arduously
And you with your sly smile
Came so gaily
Just to put another…
Yet another endless rung on it

Every sky I flew through so painstakingly
And you with your generous stroke
Came so nonchalantly
Just to paint another…
Another vast blue on it

Every road I took so eagerly
And you with your wilful intent
Came so scornfully
Just to elongate another…
Another infinite mile upon it

Every wrecked dream I shorn of
And you with your malicious heart
Came so silently
Just to give me another...
Another unfulfilled wish on it.

◆◆◆

August Night

Bamboo silhouette against the evening sky
A spiky haired ghost
The nimbus sulks
Unfallen tears and unaccepted pleas
One such August evening
The doors of my heart shut themselves.
Unasked, uninformed
The prick of the pebble under my feet
I had loved that day
On an evening like this, secretly
Leaving him behind in an unknown place
I came back to my kitchen
The flaming butane on my palm
I had loved it that night
The tears shed, the pleas accepted
The nimbus roared in exultation
Through the fissures of the thatched hut
I felt the rain drops nudging
On my cheeks
And I had loved it that night

◆◆◆

Becoming of You in Me

When you look at me
I become the most pure
When you smile at me
I become the sibling of moon
When you walk beside me
Cherubs flirt with my hair
When you inhale me
I become the scent of divinity.
Tinged with the hue of pale heaven
The trail of your thumb on my bosom
The trail from here to Mecca
That day dicing with words
I played a poem for you
Tonight your eyes dice with mine
I become the poetry itself.
This becoming of me;
This undoing of you
Is neither you nor me
This is you-becoming-in-me.

◆◆◆

Awaited One

Come!
Awaited one
On your shoulder
I shall lay my head
Silently so silently
And I have made peace with my anguish

Come!
Awaited one
The ember in the hearth is dead
Sit beside me
Silently so silently
Your warm scent wraps me

Come!
Awaited one
Pass me through this lane
As softly as feline feet
Silently so silently
Today say not a word
Hush! Be quiet
Isn't it beautiful?
To just look at each other
To feel the touch of your gaze

Isn't it beautiful?
To feel my breath on your shoulder
Isn't it beautiful to just be silent?
I am in love
With you and this quietness

◆◆◆

To My Beloved

The moment you dethrone
That goddess in your heart
And replace it with me
Allow me to know
Let me taste it with a vengeance

The day when you wish to say
'Let's go home'
I am standing by
Ready to leave everything aside
To set forth hand in hand

When you want to let yourself loose
And swim in my wave
When you want to drown yourself
In the depth of me
Drunk with me
Tell me

But never ask me where I go
In the midst of dark nights
Never ask me what I metamorphosed into
In the full moon light
Never ask me why
I vanish in those sullen evenings
Never ask me to lock my doors
You never know when my wings burst forth

Never ask me to bind my hair
For my comrades trace me through its scent
My beloved!
Never ask me my revelation.

♦♦♦

Oh! Miserable March

Oh! Miserable March
Why is spring everywhere but not in my heart?
Why is it that death always comes
And stand in front of me in March?
How couldn't I loved him?
How couldn't I?
It was a tieless knot ...
To an unnamed kingdom my love belongs
There will never be a last line for him,
Never a last sigh
Always and always in the kingdom of my dreams
He is mine
On its rugged landscape he walks free
Free at least in my dreams

♦♦♦

Shreema Ningombam

Beneath the Chattra

In one such twilight of May
When prophesy from laibung
Hums like bees in air
Fading sun languorous around your face
I wiped the sweat from your brow
Under those branches
Beside the running stream
We cast net and caught dreams
Now it's time to set them free
Once more
Into the ever running flow
Of the river of dreams, drown and lost.
Once more
You came to measure the cost of my smile
When it soars into the sky
Like a kite on endless twine
In the rain of this valley
You came and sat with me
You are gone so is the rain
Yet once more I am wet
You came
Like every day you come
Just to say "chatlage"
I tucked leihao on my ear
Once more I watch you
Recede through the laibung
You took from me
A fibre of my phanek

A wisp of my hair
A mark of my teeth on your fingers
And I sat under the Chattra
Gazing into loneliness
That flash of your departure
I become your mother and your woman
Once again

◆◆◆

Laibung: the ground where the festival of worshipping the local diety is celebrated
Chatlage: a way of saying "goodbye" in Meiteilon but in literal translation it means 'I will go now'
Leihao: an aromatic flower used by Meitei women to tuck in their hair for aesthetic purpose
Chattra: a kind of parasol offered to God

Nomads and Their Caravan

Halt the advancing dreamlets
They only show the earthly
Hold the flapping winglets
The only tempt freedom
Hold the flooding starlets
They only drown souls
Halt the ticking timelets
The past is already brimming

Halt that story teller
Who narrates my legend
I decide to join the caravans
Of nomads of this tribe
Tonight I prepare my trousseau
These dreams; these wings
These stars; these ticking times

See my groom on the horizon
He who nonchalantly walks towards me
I have not seen him ever before
But I do know his gait,
I do know his hair ruffled by fingers of wind
I do know his scent
Drifting as though from fresh bamboo grooves

I do know he is the one who should be coming
Long lost; long foretold to be found
Long time ticks away
Sand's last grain slips through my fist
Right here right now
I am a bride of all times

Chaoba Phuritshabam

To the One in Love

You waste all that on me, love
For which my soul was caged
Forgetting
The green field
Where the bird sings her heart out
The fountains
Where the soft touch of water
Tames the ego of rocky stones

You, love
You waste all that on me
Stolen springs and dreams
Too bright to last long
Hopes are too starry to shine ever
My future cries over becoming a past
My spirit stands motionless in gloom
Hovering over lies of bygones

Oh! You waste all that on me, love
All my days are gone with nightly dreams
Haunting visions amidst stars
Where your footsteps gleam
You waste all that on me, Love
Now I dwell alone
In the world of death
Where my soul is a stagnant tide

Chaoba Phuritshabam

No stars could be brighter
No moon shines more radiant
For wishes blink and lost
I rest in dead bed of flowers
Pain never comes to me now
No more tears from my eyes
My soul gives me sigh for sigh today
Yet all day I shine brighter.

◆◆◆

My Red Comrade

Morning dew on grass
My nocturnal dream:
Standing in front of the door
In the dead of the night

You try to wipe away
Woes and pains
I relive those moments
Where we belonged together
Anticipating another day
You would be calling me
From
Across the road,
Across rivers and woods

Let's walk again that path
Chosen for us
I will not deny you today
My footsteps count yours
As the time passes by
Grow old with you
As life takes a toll on me and you?
Where are you
My red comrade?

♦♦♦

Renunciation

The night passes
Reopening the cemented wound
Hidden so far
In an earthen space
Like a century old tomb

When the heart desired
To hum a forgotten song
This night
Clad with its darkness
Broke its rhythm

How I wish to conceal
Her beauty, power and wisdom tonight
So far
She only hurt me
She only tore me into pieces

You see how insensible
The trees, the stones and the flowers are
Lying unanswered to me

How numb the winds,
The moon and the stars tonight
They could never let you go
Though you silently left me long ago
As this moment passes
I'm painted with a hue

Of red
And I'm invisible
Wrap and clad with senses
Of joy and loss...

♦♦♦

Season of Love

Autumn witnesses the moment you left me
Yellow leaves fall upon melancholic lanes
Colours of March dye your last footprint
On the invisible canvas of my memory
It was when the season of love ends

Spring paid a visit after you are gone
With her green petals refreshing memories
Leaving me in a forlorn solitude
It was when the season of love ends

Winter came with its cold caressing touch
Bringing only your lost smile
Whose touch to my heart I ignored
It was when the season of love ends

Summer came and went
Only to rage me in the fire of an awakened hurt
The season of life come and goes
Though shadows still burn alive
Within walls of the dark night
It was when the season of love ends

Moon in August sky
Woke me before the night fell
Witnessing your existence within me
I cry upon this emptiness
It was when the season of love ends

◆◆◆

Untitled

Dreams are no longer dim and sad
birds cherishes
only the rhythm of my childhood songs.
Ah! The soft touch of the grass under my feet
The naughty gusts of wind playing with my hair
I'm like flowers in the breeze
Heavenly feeling of freedom…

On the starry nights of Mera
Resting my head on the lap of my mother
I shared my starry dreams

Every enthralled night
Looking for the moon and stars
Dancing in the tune of my love songs

No melancholy nights ever keep me awake
No fearful dreams of another lost
No sad songs ever echoed in my life…

◆◆◆

Mera: month of October

Rain comes Down

Rain came a decade ago, a year ago
Rain came in a gone sad day
Though it only tried to wash away his memory
Leaving me alone without his sin to carry forward
Though I complained not
For his sudden departure from my nocturnal dream
Though I did not question him
I only smiled teasing at his eroding footsteps in the sand
When the rare raindrops of winter suddenly moisten my lips
I feel your existence around me
Oh! Isn't this beginning of a new dream?

◆◆◆

Yet For Another Womb!!

Yet for another womb
Another mother
I seek from this life
Whom I can ask to embrace us
Within one womb
There we can play
Like twin embryos
Within a sheltered shell
Where their pointing fingers
Shall never pierce us

Another surname
Another clan
I seek from this world
To prove our belongingness
To the same blood

Yet for another worthless battle
Another winner-less war
I seek from this life
Just to fight and die
To test your stance for me

Yet for another womb
Yet for another mother
I seek from this life.

◆◆◆

Uncertainty

Walking on a path less known,
Believing in a truth not acceptable,
Forgetting the one closer than my soul,
This is where I have arrived,
The land which is uncertain,
Uncertainty which lies beyond me,
The path I would walk again
Uncertain to me,
Unknown and unacceptable,
Where I lost trust,
Where I cannot think beyond you!
Another uncertainty,
Waiting for me in the path ahead!
It may wrap what it wants
Without bothering me,
I have no choice to deny it,
I have to move on,
Until I reach to touch
And walk upon another uncertainty.

◆◆◆

Soibam Haripriya

Seeking an End

Is it some mere floors above?
Or perhaps at the graceful end
of a coiled rope?
Is it within the depth of a well
with its liquid blackness
calling out my name?
Is it next to the warm comfort of my bed
in a clear bottle that promises peaceful slumber?
Shall I choose the obscure hour of my birth
where the night and day met?
Shall I choose the music of raindrops
on the tin roof to bid me this farewell?
Shall I in a splash immerse myself
in the arms of an immense lake
and leave in my wake
a few ripples?

◆◆◆

A Death of My Own

Of all the things
I wish to own
I wish my death
To be my own

A quiet dignity
Of privacy
Not a grainy picture
in a newspaper
Not a being
ripped from a warm cocoon
Not a mere body
trespassed in life
trespassed beyond life

I wish not for the raging flames
to engulf me into ashes
I wish
a piece of earth
to provide me solace
in its honeyed chest
To undo the poison
This life has fed

For a flower of red
To bloom
From my navel
And a drop of dew
To adorn its petals

For the wind to play
amongst my branches
And carry in its trail
Tales of my brimming passion

For a lover to pluck my flowers
And embellish the beloved
With my petals
With my scent
With this
You will infuse
my death
with life again

◆◆◆

Time

In little meandering droplets
they slither unseen
in factions of poetry
in shards of crystals
of the boiling spring
bringing tales of the dark earth beneath

You brought me from your tales
some of your tears
I came with mine
To meet you 'tween
verses of timelessness
To forget times that left us
halfway on a broken bridge
stranded on a cliff of concrete

Slumber swallowed evenings
found us dreading the soft dusk
when the hour arrived
asking for a conclusion
to our chronology
We left with reluctance
hand in hand
to seek another time
beyond time

♦♦♦

To The Researcher

Write me love
Write me a companion
In that questionnaire you brought
Write me food, with salt and pepper and turmeric
But don't come empty handed
Just to fill up your pages
I gave you tea sweetened with sugar from my neighbours
I gave you tea sweetened with milk from my master
Yet you come just to take
A little more than what I give
Tell me
What do you write
In those pages of yours
Do you write of my suffering?
Does it make a good story?
Does it say I need everything
that everyone else needs?
Does it say I suffer everything
And I pray no one suffers the same?
Does it say my village is parched,
That my river runs and finds its way to your water taps
That my earth produces and finds its way to your kitchen
Tell me, tell me
Talk to me awhile
Not of your questions
Tell me
What lies beyond these fences of mine?
I haven't been on my feet for awhile

Listen to me
Even if they are not answers to your questions
I want to talk about
Purple skies of my youth
Though all that I have now
Is yellow winter
And you- my only visitor this year

◆◆◆

Without You

I joined the melancholic millions today-
Walking down the bottomless evening,
Colourless people in colourless clothes
Dabbled brown with life's hue.
The evening closes in—on the lifeless trees jutting out from
the sewage
Dirt poisoning their veins slowly and surely
Dry branches outstretched to its fate
I watch the sun go down behind the sewage lake
Utter blackness covering the muck.
I dusted my yellow tears stained pillows
Shut the window against the lonesome sight.
I wait for the day the rains would visit –house by house
Cleanse the coating of dirt and death;
Mingle with the earthy aroma
While evening drips down our shared umbrella.

◆◆◆

Prayers

My promiscuous hair
Bound in a tight knot
Veiled from my Etei
Lest the scent of Chenghi
Wafts towards him
Enhanced by the earthy smell of slight cowdung
Effusing from the moist chakravyuh
Marked by the span of my arms
Around the silent scented tulsi

Unbelieving
Atheist
I prayed twice a day
With incense, water and flowers
For the heavens to drop
A thick noose
Knotted with sudden stars
With the moon for an audience
To witness my escape
From this Chakravyuh

◆◆◆

Etei: elder brother in law, In Meitei culture a woman should
cover her head if she sees her elder brother in law.
Chenghi: a traditional liquid mixture of rice water and herbs
used for rinsing hair
Chakravyuh: a circular labyrinth

Remnants

Just a whiff remains
of your sweat
besides my pillow
where you wept in ecstasy

Just a strand remains
tangled amongst my fingers
which ruffled tenderly
dark clouds of new moon

Just a moan remains
of your voice
bleeding amongst wounds
raging amongst fires
muffled amongst kisses
honeyed amongst songs
salted amongst tears
Leafless in autumn
And naked in winter

♦♦♦

Soibam Haripriya

I will Take the Leap

Just a peep
Is what I ask for
Into the beyond
Seconds of that image
Whether tongues of flame
Whether serenity of cold blue light
Whether nothing and nothing
Is the knowledge
I desire
to stab my womb
to stop my blood
From furthering itself
into oblivion
of the sole truth
and its multi fanged friends
My blood
My flesh
Let me stab you
Here itself
In the warmth
Of my fluid
Before life
And its many brutes
Play their games
Let me stab me
Stab me along with you
I will be with you
In the arms of beyond

Whether heaven and its precocious morality
Whether hell and its overwhelming temptation
Whether the erasure of nothingness
I will take the leap

◆◆◆

Footsteps

Lavender sky
Before the gold
Then the deep impenetrable evenings
Warm glow from houses
Sends a shiver down my spine
I returned to a dark house
Waiting for me
In the dark inkiness I waited
September came and left
I waited on

Partaking shivering cold dinner
in my bed,
Time indifferent of me
ticked endlessly
Each morning I strike off a day
In the Manipuri- English calendar
Tattered during transit
The calendar showing *thasi* and *purnima*;
when not to travel north

I gazed at the calendar
Hoping to revive-
An acoustic memory
Of footsteps against the wooden staircase
A soft thud and the sound ascending
Hesitating, a tense lingering silence
A footstep that stops to knock
Stops at my door.

♦♦♦

Thasi: new moon
Purnima: new moon

Soibam Haripriya

My Wayward Sibling

My wayward sibling
Sudden in arrivals
Abrupt in departure
Promptly came
On days hard as stone
Unwrapped
fistful of woes
I survived lovers'
goodbyes
To eternity
He took me
for rainwashed walks
He opened the day
to the scent of frangipani
Now he leaves
His goodbye
gnaws the evening

◆◆◆

About the Authors

Chaoba Phuritshabam is a post graduate in Chemistry from Miranda House, Delhi University and an LLB from the Faculty of Law, Delhi University. She currently works in the field of Intellectual Property law. She also occasionally dabbles with journalism and had reported for the Imphal-based Sangai Express as their Delhi Correspondent in 2006-2008. Some of her poems have been featured in a journal of poetry, Our Private Literature, published by Burning Voices.

Shreema Ningombam is currently an Assistant Professor (Political Science) in Nambol L. Sanoi College, Manipur. She completed her M. Phil from the Department of Political Science, University of Delhi in 2009 and availed the Teaching Assistant Fellowship in the same Department. Her poems have been published in Muse India as well as in Our Private Literature, published by Burning Voices. Her current research area is sexuality of women.

Soibam Haripriya is a doctoral candidate at the Department of Sociology, Delhi School of Economics, University of Delhi. She completed her M Phil from the same department. She is an Assistant Professor in the Gender Studies Department, Ambedkar University, Delhi. Her poems have been published in The Sangai Express and Our Private Literature. Haripriya has a keen interest in documenting and analysing changing meaning of "sites" in the cultural landscape of Manipur.

Printed in the United States
By Bookmasters